MAJOR LEAGUE SOCCER

BY DAVID RAUSCH

BELLWETHER MEDIA • MINNEAPOLIS, MN

EPIC BOOKS are no ordinary books. They burst with intense action, high-speed heroics, and shadows of the unknown. Are you ready for an Epic adventure?

This edition first published in 2015 by Bellwether Media, Inc.

No part of this publication may be reproduced in whole or in part without written permission of the publisher. For information regarding permission, write to Bellwether Media, Inc., Attention: Permissions Department, 5357 Penn Avenue South, Minneapolis, MN 55419.

Library of Congress Cataloging-in-Publication Data

Rausch, David.
  Major League Soccer / by David Rausch.
    pages cm. – (Epic: Major League Sports)
  Includes bibliographical references and index.
  Summary: "Engaging images accompany information about Major League Soccer. The combination of high-interest subject matter and light text is intended for students in grades 2 through 7"– Provided by publisher.
  ISBN 978-1-62617-134-3 (hardcover : alk. paper)
  1. Major League Soccer (Organization)–Juvenile literature. 2. Soccer–United States–Juvenile literature. I. Title.
  GV944.U5R38 2014
  796.334'64–dc23
                    2014010777

Printed in the United States of America, North Mankato, MN.

TABLE OF CONTENTS

WHAT IS MLS?

Major **League** Soccer (MLS) is a **professional** soccer league in the United States and Canada. Players from around the world play in MLS.

HISTORY OF MLS

In 1994, the U.S. hosted the **FIFA World Cup**. The U.S. received this honor after promising to start a pro league. MLS played its first season two years later.

NORTH AMERICAN SOCCER LEAGUE

There were other pro leagues in the U.S. before MLS. The North American Soccer League played from 1967 to 1984.

MLS had ten **clubs** in its first season. Since then, it has doubled in size. It is quickly growing more popular.

First MLS game, 1996

A LOOK BACK

1950: The National Soccer Hall of Fame forms.

December 1967: The National American Soccer League forms.

1984: The National American Soccer League plays its last season.

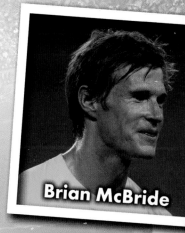

December 17, 1993: Major League Soccer forms.

February 6, 1996: MLS has its first draft. Brian McBride is the first player drafted.

July 14, 1996: The first MLS All-Star Game is played.

Brian McBride

October 20, 1996: D.C. United beats the Los Angeles Galaxy to win the first MLS championship game.

April 9, 1997: MLS adds two new clubs for the first time. They are the Chicago Fire and Miami Fusion.

January 11, 2007: The L.A. Galaxy signs world superstar David Beckham.

David Beckham

THE CLUBS

MLS is a growing league. The 2014 season had 19 clubs divided between the Eastern and Western **Conferences**. The 2015 season welcomes 2 new clubs.

EASTERN CONFERENCE

- **Chicago Fire**
- **Columbus Crew**
- **D.C. United**
- **Houston Dynamo**
- **Montreal Impact**
- **New England Revolution**
- **New York Red Bulls**
- **Philadelphia Union**
- **Sporting Kansas City**
- **Toronto FC**

WESTERN CONFERENCE

- **Chivas USA**
- **Colorado Rapids**
- **FC Dallas**
- **Los Angeles Galaxy**
- **Portland Timbers**
- **Real Salt Lake**
- **San Jose Earthquakes**
- **Seattle Sounders FC**
- **Vancouver Whitecaps**

Added in 2015: New York City FC and Orlando City SC

Each club has 18 players on its **game day roster**. Clubs **draft** young players to build their roster. They also sign **free agents** and trade with other clubs.

MLS draft

ROSTER LIMITS

A roster can have up to eight players from other countries.

PLAYING THE GAME

Clubs score by moving the ball into the net. A soccer game has two 45-minute periods. **Referees** call **fouls** when rules are broken.

OVERTIME

A tie game goes into overtime. Clubs then play two 15-minute periods. They have penalty kicks if neither club scores.

SOCCER TALK

corner kick—when a player kicks the ball in-bounds from the corner of the field

dribble—when a player moves the ball forward with the feet while running

goal—when a player shoots the ball into the net; 1 point

header—when a player hits the ball with his head

pass—when a player moves the ball to another player

penalty kick—when a player gets a free kick at the goal against the opponent's goalie

save—when the goalie blocks a shot that would have scored a goal

steal—when a player takes the ball away from another player

THE REGULAR SEASON

Clubs begin training camp in late January. Players prepare for the 34 regular season games. The season runs from March through October.

THE SUPPORTERS' SHIELD

Clubs earn points for each win and tie in the season. The club with the most points wins the Supporters' Shield award.

THE PLAYOFFS AND THE MLS CUP

The top five clubs from each conference make the playoffs. Each conference has a **knockout** round first. Then **semifinals** and **finals** decide conference champions.

ADD 'EM UP!

One club beats another by scoring more points in a round.

The conference champions face off in the MLS Cup. The winners celebrate with the Philip F. Anschutz Trophy. They are the best in the league!

GLOSSARY

clubs—teams in MLS

conferences—groups of sports teams within a league; teams in a conference often play one another.

draft—to choose young players to join MLS

FIFA World Cup—a world soccer tournament of national teams

finals—the playoff round that determines the conference champions

fouls—plays and actions that break the rules

free agents—professional athletes who are free to play for any team; free agents are not under a contract.

game day roster—a list of players on a team who can play in an MLS game

knockout—the playoff round that determines which teams make it to the conference semifinals

league—a group of people or teams united by a common interest or activity

professional—a level where athletes get paid to play a sport

referees—people who enforce the rules during a game

semifinals—the playoff round that determines which teams compete for the conference championships

TO LEARN MORE

At the Library

Doeden, Matt. *The World's Greatest Soccer Players*. Mankato, Minn.: Capstone Press, 2010.

Forest, Christopher. *Play Soccer Like a Pro: Key Skills and Tips*. Mankato, Minn.: Capstone Press, 2011.

Hornby, Hugh. *Soccer*. New York, N.Y.: DK, 2010.

On the Web

Learning more about Major League Soccer is as easy as 1, 2, 3.

1. Go to www.factsurfer.com.

2. Enter "Major League Soccer" into the search box.

3. Click the "Surf" button and you will see a list of related web sites.

With factsurfer.com, finding more information is just a click away.

INDEX

The images in this book are reproduced through the courtesy of: Tyson Hofsommer/ ZUMA Press/ Corbis, front cover (left); Nick Turchiaro/ isiphotos/ Corbis, front cover (top right); George Holland/ Cal Sport Media/ Newscom, pp. 4-5; Mark Leech/ Offside/ Corbis, p. 6; George Tiedemann/ Corbis, p. 7; Associated Press, pp. 8, 21; SMI/ Newscom, p. 9 (top); Ira L. Black/ Corbis, p. 9 (bottom); Howard C. Smith/ isiphotos/ Corbis, p. 10; Andy Mead/ YCJ/ Icon SML/ Corbis, p. 12; Ted S. Warren/ AP/ Corbis, pp. 13, 16-17; Don Ryan/ AP/ Corbis, p. 14; Fred Kfoury/ Icon SML/ Corbis, p. 15; Michael Janosz/ ISI/ Corbis, p. 19; John Sleezer/ MCT/ Newscom, p. 20.